# JOINT RAILWAYS EASTERN AND SOUTHERN ENGLAND

Patrick Bennett

AMBERLEY

First published 2025

Amberley Publishing
The Hill, Stroud
Gloucestershire, GL5 4EP

www.amberley-books.com



ISBN 978 1 3981 1935 2 (print)
ISBN 978 1 3981 1936 9 (ebook)



British Library Cataloguing in Publication Data.
A catalogue record for this book is available from the British Library.

Origination by Amberley Publishing.
Printed in the UK.

Appointed GPSR EU Representative: Easy Access System Europe Oü, 16879218
Address: Mustamäe tee 50, 10621, Tallinn, Estonia
Contact Details: gpsr.requests@easproject.com, +358 40 500 3575

# Contents

# Introduction

Despite being fiercely competitive, the pre-Grouping railway companies did, on a number of occasions when it served their mutual interest, collaborate in the building or owning of railway lines. These lines could be as minor as the 4 miles between Epsom and Leatherhead, shared by the London & South Western Railway and the London & Brighton, or as large as a complete railway system such as the Midland & Great Northern. As far as the former is concerned, it has to be said that despite sharing the track, each company insisted on having its own stations at both Epsom and Leatherhead!

The three great joint companies were the Cheshire Lines Committee, the Midland & Great Northern, and the Somerset & Dorset. The M&GN and the S&D had their own locomotives and rolling stock, while the motive power of the CLC was supplied by the Great Central Railway. Sadly, the M&GN and the S&D are no longer with us but happily the CLC survives almost in its entirety. These three companies survived as independent concerns up to Nationalisation, although in their later years increasingly came under the control of the owning companies.

Far more numerous than these independent concerns were the lines which had no rolling stock of their own but the usage of which was shared between the parent companies. Often these lines were shared between just two companies, the Great Northern & Great Eastern Joint is a good example, but occasionally there were multiple owning companies. The South Yorkshire Joint was owned by no less than five. The story of these lines, how they came into being under joint ownership and, sadly, in the case of some of them how they were closed is recounted here.

The publisher and author would like to thank Peter Groom for permission to use photographs taken at Melton Mowbray and Saxby; Peter Lovell for the photographs taken at Princes Risborough, High Wycombe, and Saunderton; and the Branch Line Society for permission to use photographs by Angus McDougall taken at Melton Constable and Princes Risborough. The photographs by Ben Brooksbank, Alan Murray-Rust, Geoffrey Skelsey, Lamberhurst, sunil060902, Martin Addison, and Dr Neil Clifton are reproduced under the Creative-Commons Share-Alike Licence 2.0. Every attempt has been made to seek permission for copyright material in this book. However, if we have inadvertently used copyright material without permission or acknowledgement, we apologise and will make the necessary correction at the first opportunity.

# The Great Northern & Great Eastern Joint Line

The GER had for a long time wished to penetrate GNR territory, not least to participate in the lucrative Yorkshire coal traffic. Finally, after thirty years of battling with the GN, in 1879 an agreement was reached to operate a joint line from Huntingdon to Doncaster, via March and Lincoln. The new joint line incorporated sections of railway that had already been built. These were Huntingdon to March built by the ECR/EAR between 1847 and 1851 and the GNR lines from Spalding to March (1867), Pyewipe Junction to Gainsborough (1849), and Gainsborough to Doncaster (1867). The branch from Somersham to Ramsey East, which opened in 1889, was also included. The new section of railway needed to complete the line, from Spalding to Pyewipe Junction, was opened in August 1882, at which time the joint committee took over the management of the line. Five directors were appointed from each company. Responsibility for the line was divided. North of March work was carried out by the GN, and south thereof by the GE.

In 1906, there were eight express trains daily between March and Doncaster, as well as eleven scheduled coal trains, and seven daily mixed goods. There were three GE expresses daily between Liverpool Street and York. These did not survive the First World War but the daily Harwich–York boat train did. In 1934 there were through carriages between Harwich and both Liverpool and York. There were also York–Lowestoft, Ipswich–Sheffield, and Yarmouth–Leeds trains, as well as five Up and four Down stopping trains between March and Doncaster.

In 1960, on the joint line there were still trains between King's Cross and Lincoln, Colchester and Newcastle, Yarmouth and York, and the boat train between Liverpool and Harwich. On Sundays there was a Leeds to Norwich service. Stopping trains ran between Lincoln and Sheffield, Lincoln and Doncaster, and March and Doncaster. The Ramsey branch lost its passenger service in 1930, and the March–St Ives line closed in 1967, with the St Ives–Huntingdon line having previously closed in 1959. The March–Spalding passenger service ended on 11 September 1961, and the line closed completely in 1982.

Of the original thirty-three stations on the joint line just seven remain open. There were numerous signal boxes; in 1988 there were still twenty but today just three control the line. Following the closure of the March–Spalding section of the line in 1982 trains are now routed to/from Peterborough.

Between 2012 and 2015 a major upgrade of the joint line was carried out. The purpose of this was to raise the line speed from 60 to 75 mph and increase the loading gauge to W10 in order to allow the line to be used as a diversionary route by intermodal trains. In the event, the loading gauge was increased to W12. The work involved the closure of thirteen manual signal boxes, upgrading more than sixty level crossings, relaying of track, and the replacement of numerous bridges. The Sleaford avoiding line was rebuilt to double track. The joint line is also used as a diversionary route for passenger trains. Today there is just a local passenger service, consisting of nine trains each way between Lincoln and Peterborough and five between Peterborough and Doncaster. There is no Sunday service.

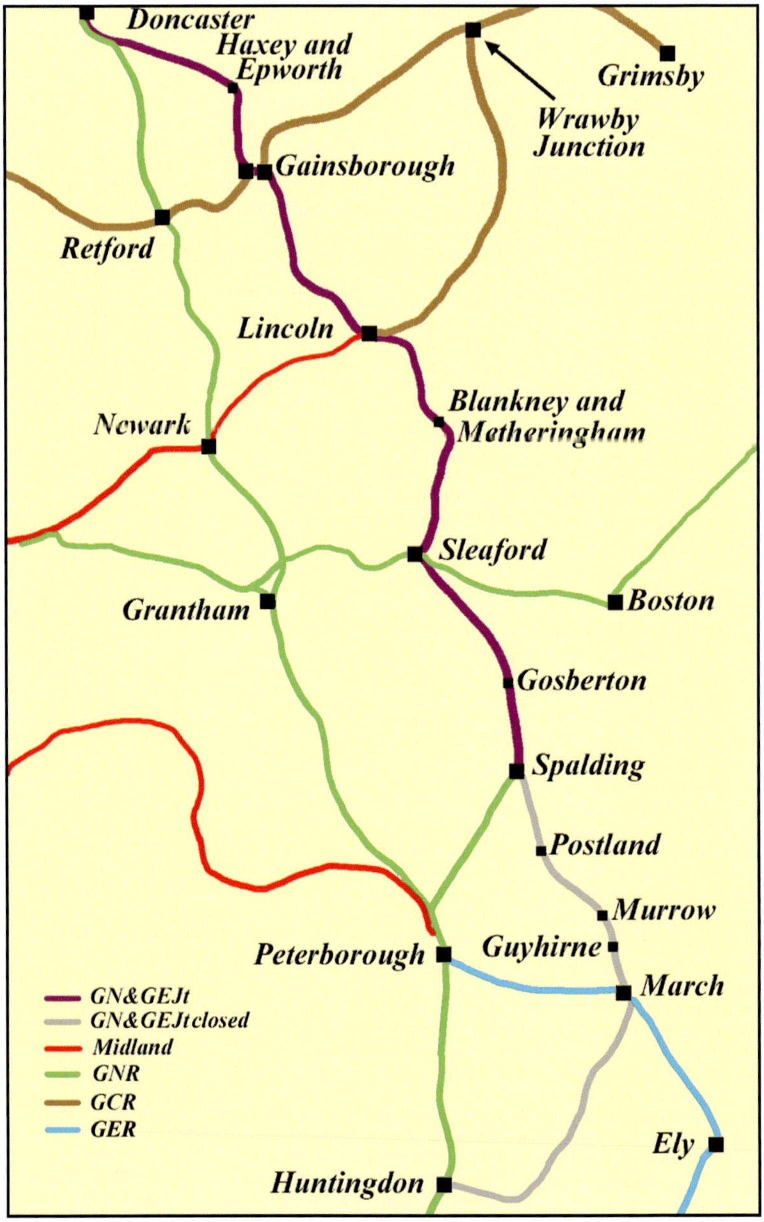


The joint line.

Huntingdon Joint station opened in 1883. It became Huntingdon East in 1923. This is a view form the east, taken from the signal box. The GN main line is over to the left.

Godmanchester was originally Huntingdon. The name change came about with the opening of the joint station. Standing at the signal box in the 1950s is J15 No. 65457. This Cambridge engine, built in 1906, became one of the last of the class to be withdrawn, succumbing in 1962.

St Ives was effectively at the junction of four lines, from Cambridge, March, Ely, and Kettering. Despite this apparent utility, it lost its last passenger service on 5 October 1970. A scene from the 1950s. Next to the engine is a Siphon wagon, used to transport milk in churns.

The line from Wisbech to St Ives was built by the Wisbech, St Ives & Cambridge Junction Railway, shortly to be part of the Eastern Counties Railway. The southern section, which included the stations of Wimblington, Chatteris, and Somersham, opened on 1 February 1848. Somersham station is seen in 1973, six years after closure. (Geoffrey Skelsey)

The Ramsey branch opened on 16 September 1889 and on 1 January 1897 was transferred to the GN & GEJt committee. Warboys station is seen shortly after opening with an Adams '61 Class' 0-4-4T in attendance. Note the wooden board fitted to enable bunker-first running. These locomotives were later fitted with full cabs.

Ramsey is seen in the 1920s. The locomotive is F7 2-4-2 No. 8302. The Ramsey branch lost its passenger service in 1930, while freight lingered on until 1964.

The view north at Chatteris in the 1960s. In 1960 Chatteris had a service of six return services on weekdays with two additional trains on Wednesdays and Saturdays. On Sundays there were four Down trains and three Up. (Lamberhurst)

Wimblington station looking north. Like the other stations on the line, Wimblington lost its passenger service on 6 March 1967.

On 18 April 1990 Class 31 Nos 31327 and 31326 pass March East Junction signal box with a westbound Freightliner service. The leading locomotive is in the early 'Red Stripe' Railfreight livery.

A view north at Guyhirn, showing its rudimentary facilities. Even today Guyhirn is a tiny settlement, so little surprise that it lost its passenger service as early as 1953.

The next station north was Murrow, where the GN/GE line crossed the M&GN Peterborough–Sutton line on the flat. This signal box was a replacement, built after an earlier one was demolished by a collision between two freight trains in 1925. Seen here in 1990, it was later rebuilt as a private dwelling.

There wasn't really a settlement a Postland at all. The station was situated where the railway crossed a road. In 1922 just four trains a day called.

Spalding was once an important junction, the meeting point of lines from March, Peterborough, Bourne, Sleaford, Boston, and Sutton. The empty platforms seen on 15 July 1989 give an idea of its former importance.

In 1960 O1 2-8-0 No. 63803 stands at Spalding. This was a Thompson rebuild of a Robinson 04. The clue to its origin is the GC tender. (Lamberhurst)

Gosberton was one of the new stations which came into being when the stretch of line between Spalding and Pyewipe Junction opened in 1882. It closed to passengers on 11 September 1961 and to freight on 5 October 1964. On 20 June 1991 Class 47 No. 47332 approaches Gosberton 100 crossing with a short engineering train. The closed station buildings can be seen to the left of the locomotive. In the background is Gosberton signal box. This signal box was closed and replaced by a new modular box at Gosberton 100 crossing. This too has now closed and the line here is now controlled from Lincoln SCC.

On 2 June 1989 a Metro-Cammell Class 101 unit passes Sleaford East signal box as it enters the station with a Skegness–Doncaster service. At one time Sleaford had North, South, East and West boxes. Today only the West and East boxes survive. The latter dates from 1882 and is a Grade II listed building.

A staff photograph taken at Ruskington. Interestingly, even some of the permanent-way staff are wearing ties and none of the men is without a hat. Ruskington closed in 1961 but reopened along with Metheringham in 1975.

Blankney and Metheringham station also opened with the new section of the joint line. It closed in 1961 but was reopened in 1975 as Metheringham. The signal box retained the name Blankney. It is a rare GNR Type 4 box, despite actually being built by the LNER. For this reason and its largely original condition it is a listed building. It lost its status as a block post in 2014 but has been retained in use to work the crossing barriers, which have now replaced the gates seen in this photograph from 1989.

Nocton and Dunston was one of the stations opened with the new section of line from Spalding to Pyewipe Junction. All were built in a similar style.

Of the original thirty-three stations on the joint line just seven remain open. There were numerous signal boxes; in 1988 there were still twenty but today just three control the line. Following the closure of the March–Spalding section of the line in 1982 trains are now routed to/from Peterborough. Potterhanworth, one of the now closed signal boxes, seen in 1989. The box was a GNR Type 1 and dated from 1883.

In the 1930s Robinson B5 4-6-0 No. 5185 pulls into Potterhanworth station. The station closed on 2 May 1955.

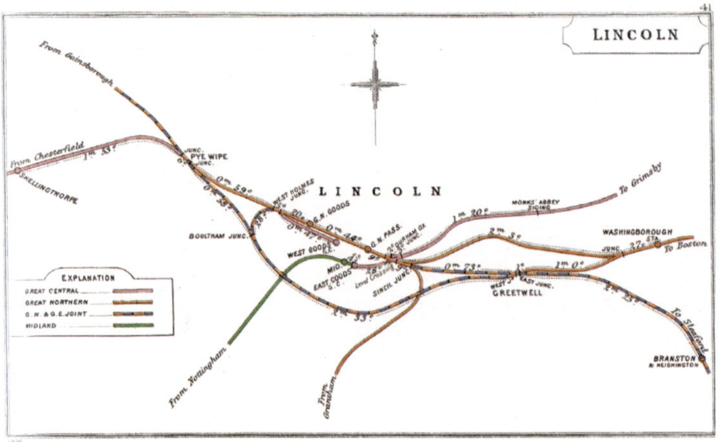


This Clearing House map shows that joint-line trains could access Lincoln from both east and west, as well as avoiding it altogether.

In the last few months of the LNER, B1 4-6-0 No. 1077 is seen at Lincoln Central on 14 April 1947. (Ben Brooksbank)

On 20 November 2021 the rail-head treatment train is seen approaching Saxilby station topped and tailed by a pair of Class 66 locomotives.

At Saxilby Class 47 No. 47770 passes the signal box hauling a diverted southbound East Coast Main Line train on 30 August 1998. The signal box was closed in 2014.

It is no longer necessary for diverted ECML trains to be loco-hauled as these Azuma units can rely on their diesel engines, as is the case with this southbound service passing through Gainsborough Lea Road on 20 November 2021.

# The Axholme Joint Line

The Goole & Marshland Light Railway was authorised in 1898 to build a line from Marshland Junction, on the Doncaster–Goole line, to Adlingfleet via Easton, with branches to Swinefleet and Luddington. In the following year the Isle of Axholme Light Railway was authorised to build a line from Haxey, where it would connect with the GN&GEJt, to Reedness Junction, where it would connect with the G&MLR. Construction was under way when both lines were purchased jointly by the NER and the L&Y, becoming the Isle of Axholme Joint Railway. Fockerby was the terminus of the branch from Reedness Junction. It was originally named Garthorpe. On the branch there were stations at Eastoft and Luddington. The line never did reach Adlingsfleet.

In 1922, there were three trains daily each way between Goole and Haxey Junction, with the same number on the Fockerby branch. There were additional services on Mondays, Wednesdays, Fridays, and Saturdays. There was no Sunday service. Trains were worked by the L&Y, mainly with Barton Wright 0-6-2Ts and Aspinall 0-6-0s and 2-4-2Ts. The LMS introduced a Sentinel railcar in 1926 and a larger one in 1930, which saw out the remaining years of the passenger service. More important was goods traffic, which consisted principally of agricultural produce as well as peat.

Haxey and Epworth station is seen in a photograph probably dating from around the end of the nineteenth century.

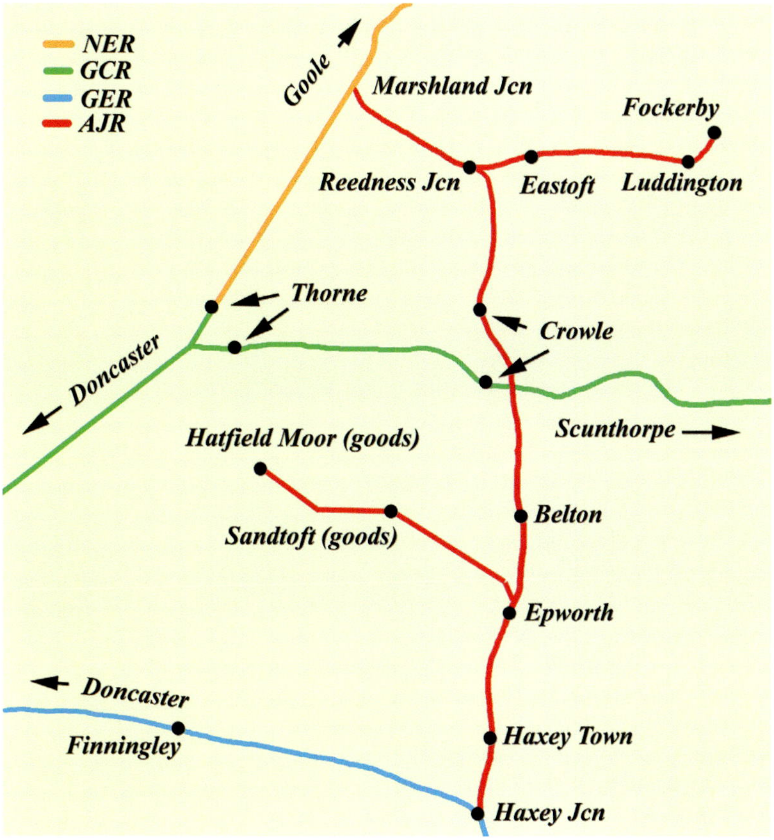


Axholme Joint Railway.

The photograph shows the opening ceremony on 2 January 1905. The Manning Wardle tank was one of the contractors' locomotives. *Halkon* was named after the chairman of the G&MLR.

Reedness Junction. The line to the left is the Fockerby branch and that to the right is the 'main line' to Haxey Junction. On the moors near here and also on Hatfield Moor were 3-foot-gauge railway systems for transporting peat, which was later moved by the IAJR.

In pre-Grouping days an L&Y 0-6-0T, train, and crew stand at Fockerby having their picture taken.

Crowle Town looking north. Notice how busy the goods yard is.

One of the Barton Wright 0-6-2Ts is seen at Haxey Junction. These engines, introduced in 1880, were the first of that wheel arrangement in Britain.

One of the major features of the railway was Crowle Swing Bridge, constructed at a cost of £20,000 by the Cleveland Bridge and Engineering Company Limited. The 102-foot-long bridge was worked by a Crossley oil engine. The bridge was dismantled but the engine has been saved. The bridge is seen here in the 1960s. A Class 47 diesel is heading along the Thorne–Wrawby Junction line.

Another feature of the line is this viaduct crossing at Folly Foot and South Engine drains.

Haxey Town station, originally named Haxey Central. The latter title was probably justified as the IALR station was considerably nearer to the village than the GCR station of Haxey and Epworth. On the IALR to the north of Epworth the Hatfield goods line branched off. This was not completed until 1909. There were goods stations at Sandtoft and Hatfield Moors.

A view of both Haxey Junction and Haxey and Epworth stations. Haxey Junction is on the left.

# The Midland & Great Northern Joint Railway

## Western Developments

The M&GN came into existence in 1893 as a result of the amalgamation of a number of smaller companies, although this did not happen overnight and the first of the railways which eventually constituted part of the system was constructed in the 1850s. The Norwich & Spalding Railway was authorised in August 1853 to build a line from Spalding to Sutton Bridge, and from there to Wisbech. The 7½-mile section as far as Holbeach opened in 1858. There were stations at Weston, Moulton, and Whaplode. It was worked by the Great Northern. A further 8 miles to Sutton Bridge opened on 1 July 1862, with stations at Fleet, Gedney, and Long Sutton.

The Peterborough, Wisbech & Sutton Bridge Railway received its authorising Act on 28 July 1863. It opened its 27-mile single-track railway throughout in 1866. There were stations at Eye Green, Thorney, Wryde, Murrow, Wisbech St Mary, Wisbech, Ferry, and Tydd. Passenger services were provided by the Midland Railway. The Lynn & Sutton Bridge Railway was authorised in August 1861, opened to goods trains in November 1864 but not until March 1866 for passenger trains. The 9½-mile-long Spalding & Bourne, with stations at North Drove, Counter Drain, and Twenty, opened on 1 August 1866. The naming of stations after water features provides the clue that the railway passed nowhere near any villages. On 23 July 1866 the L&SB and the S&B amalgamated to form the Midland & Eastern Railway, to be worked jointly by the MR and GN. The following year the N&S was leased by the M&E, being absorbed in 1877. The company was known as the Bourne & Lynn.

## Eastern Developments

The Lynn & Fakenham Railway was authorised on 13 July 1876, while the Great Yarmouth & Stalham received its Act on the 26th of the same month. Work on the latter began on the 15 January the following year. The 17¾-mile single-track line was opened in stages, being completed to Stalham by 3 July 1880. An Act of 27 May 1878 authorised a 7-mile extension to North Walsham and a change of name to the Yarmouth & North Norfolk Railway.

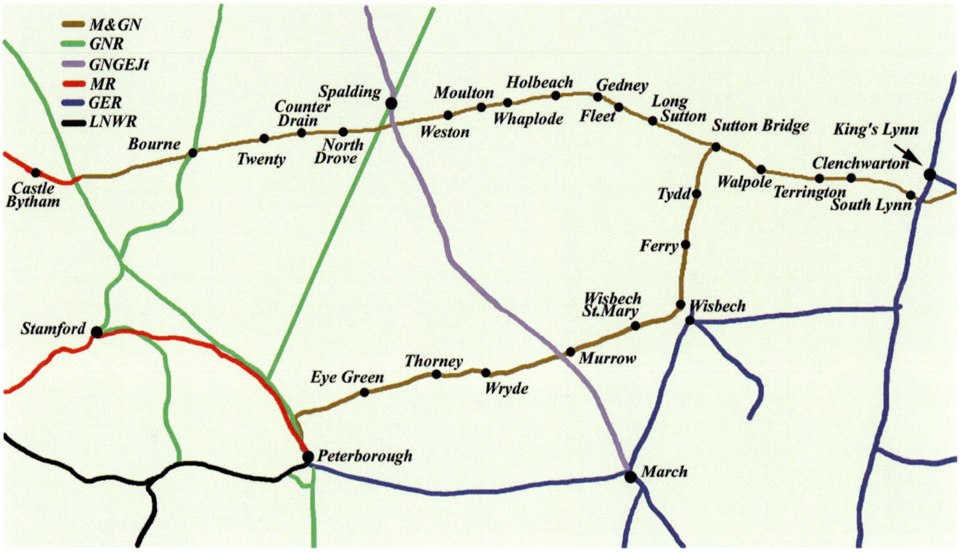


M&GN western area.

A station named after a drain, Twenty, opened as part of the Spalding & Bourne Railway on 1 August 1866. In 1893 the line between Bourne and Twenty was doubled, giving the station a second platform and a signal box. Twenty closed to passengers in 1959 but remained open for freight until 30 March 1964. Note the token catcher on the left.

Until the Spalding avoiding line opened all M&GN trains had to call at Spalding and effect a reversal. Seen here some time after 1906 is one of the Johnson 4-4-0s introduced in 1894. These engines were the main express passenger motive power until the takeover by the LNER in 1936.

The Norwich & Spalding Railway opened its line from Spalding to Holbeach on 15 November 1858. The company ran into financial difficulties and it was to be another four years before the line on to Sutton Bridge was completed. The line here was single track but Holbeach became a crossing place in 1891. The locomotive at the head of the train is a Beyer Peacock 4-4-0 dating from the 1880s.

The N&SR opened the line from Holbeach to Sutton Bridge on 1 July 1862. The station seen here replaced an earlier one further south and was opened on 1 March 1866. It became a junction with the arrival of the line from Peterborough and Wisbech on 1 August the same year.

The Crosskeys swing bridge was the third to be built across the Nene. It was completed in 1897 at a cost of £80,000. It was a combined road and rail bridge. It is still in use today as a road bridge. The bell on the signal box was rung when the bridge was about to be opened for river traffic.

At South Lynn in LMS days stands Johnson 3P 4-4-0 No. 758. Built in 1904, this engine was scrapped as No. 30758 in 1951.

On 12 April 1995 one of the last vestiges of the M&GN is removed. These are the exchange sidings at South Lynn.

A photo of Eye Green station taken before the First World War. By the end of that conflict the station name had 'for Crowland' added. The brickworks were clearly an important customer for the railway.

At Wisbech St Mary J3 0-6-0 No. 4154 arrives with a pick-up freight.

Fruit traffic was a very important source of revenue for the M&GN. Trains composed of up to sixty wagons of fruit could be seen at the height of the season. In 1936 300,000 baskets of fruit were dispatched. At Wisbech Sharp Stewart 4-4-0 No. 42 waits to depart with a trainload of fruit.

Tydd station was nowhere near either Tydd St Mary or Tydd Gate. The nearest settlement was Foul Anchor. In the 1950s 'Flying Pig' 4MT 2-6-0 No. 43156 waits to depart with an eastbound service. The shed plate indicates that this was a Melton engine.

The extension to North Walsham opened on 13 June 1881. The Lynn & Fakenham opened the first section of its line, to Massingham, on 16 August 1879, and to Fakenham on 6 August 1880. Apart from Massingham, there were stations at Grimston Road, Hillington, Rudham, and Raynham Park. The station at Fakenham was given the name Town despite being half a mile from the town centre. The initial passenger service was of six trains daily in each direction, taking between fifty-five minutes and one hour.

An Act of 12 August 1880 authorised the L&F to extend its line to Norwich via Melton Constable. The same Act authorised a branch to Blakeney Harbour. The L&F and the Y&NN saw the sense in joining their two railways by a line between Melton and North Walsham. The authorising Act, passed on 11 August 1881, also included permission to build a branch from Kelling to Cromer. The line to Norwich was opened to Guestwick on 19 January 1882, to Lenwade on 1 July, and to Norwich on 12 December the same year. The terminus was at Norwich City station.

An Act of 18 August 1882 provided for the creation of the Eastern & Midlands Railway. On 1 January 1883, the L&F, the Y&NN, and the YU would merge, to be followed six months later by the M&E and the PW&SB. In the latter cases, however, the GN and MR would continue to operate these lines within the existing agreements.

The 17-mile line between North Walsham and Melton opened on 5 April 1883. Intermediate stations were Corpusty, Aylsham, and Flemingham. Melton to Holt opened on 1 October 1884 and Holt to Cromer on 16 June 1887. The 4½-mile Lynn Loop, the Lynn avoiding line, opened on 1 January 1886. There were new stations at Gayton Road and South Lynn, the latter previously only a goods station. A goods station was created at Hardwick Road. West Lynn station closed. At this time the Blakeney branch was abandoned. The construction of a branch from North Walsham to Mundesley was authorised on 20 June 1988. The Act of 24 June 1889 authorised the construction of the line from Bourne to Saxby, and at the same time the transfer of the western section of the E&M to become the joint property of the MR and GN, for the administration of which a joint committee was established.

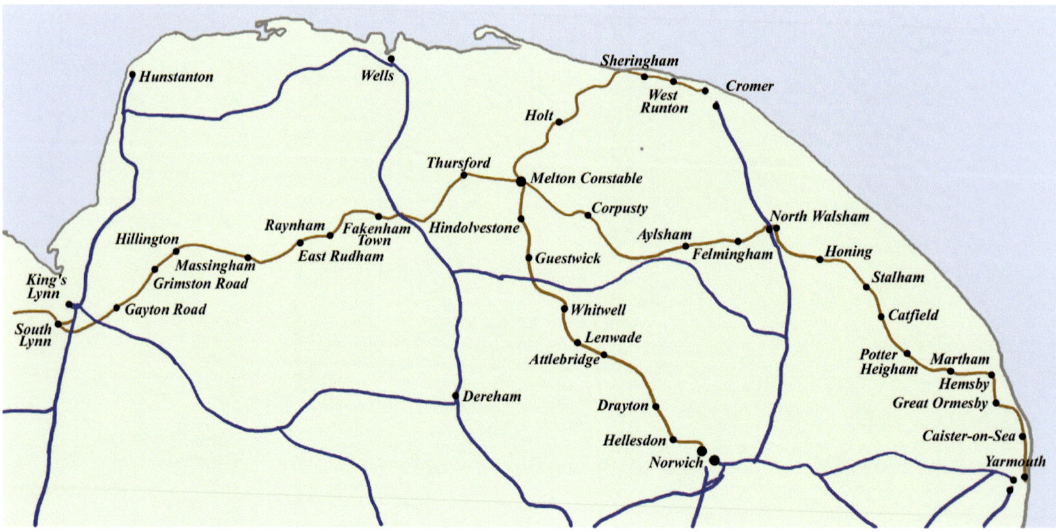


M&GN eastern area.

The bridge over the Welland to the east of Spalding. West of here was Welland Bank Junction, the starting point of the avoiding line to Cuckoo Junction, which was completed in May 1893. The bridge over the Welland dates from that time. There were signal boxes at both ends of the bridge.

In the early 1890s, the GN and MR had expressed an interest in acquiring the remainder of the E&M system. After negotiations it was agreed that this would take place and to that end an Act was passed on 9 June 1893. On 1 July 1893, the E&M was vested in the M&GN joint committee, which became the owners of 113 miles of railway, as well as thirty-nine engines, 104 carriages, 718 wagons, and five miscellaneous vehicles. Under the new arrangements the MR became responsible for the motive power side, while the GN became responsible for the permanent way and signalling. William Marriott became resident engineer and locomotive superintendent.

## The Joint Committee

The Bourne–Saxby line opened on 1 May 1894, the M&GN's portion being the 5 miles from Bourne to Little Bytham. The Spalding avoiding line opened on the same day. Work on the Mundesley branch started in December 1896 and a further Act passed in 1897 gave the M&GN powers to extend to Runton East Junction, thus giving access to Cromer Beach station. The GE and M&GN were in competition over the building of lines to serve the north-east Norfolk coast. Eventually, it was agreed to form a joint committee to build and manage the two lines: North Walsham to Cromer, and Lowestoft to Yarmouth via Gorleston. As part of these arrangements the M&GN was to build a new line from Caister Road Junction, on the Yarmouth Union Railway, to the East Suffolk Line. This would include the Breydon Viaduct. The Norfolk & Suffolk Joint Railways Committee was established by an Act of 25 July 1898.

This is Clay Lake Crossing and signal box. Notice the colour light signals with a splitting distant. Clay Lake was the next box from Welland Junction and start of the single-line section to Sutton Bridge. When Clay Lake cleared, the top head would show green, but the distant signals below would both light up and show yellow. When Welland Junction cleared, the distant signal for the route to the right or left would clear to green.

A festive day at Hillington. Clearly an important arrival is expected. Interestingly, the sign says 'for Sandringham'. The more usual station for royals bound for Sandringham was Wolferton.

Beyer-Peacock 4-4-0 No. 34 stands at Melton Constable. These engines were supplied to the Eastern & Midlands Railway between 1886 and 1888. The whole class was rebuilt with Midland boilers between 1895 and 1909.

On the last day of passenger services on the M&GN, 28 February 1959, 'Flying Pig' 4MT 2-6-0 No. 43150 stands at Melton Constable. (BLS)

At Weybourne in June 2022 on the preserved North Norfolk Railway WD 8F 2-10-0 No. 90775 waits to leave with a train to Holt.

A Class 'A' Beyer-Peacock 4-4-0 stands at Sheringham with a westbound freight. These locomotives were bought by the Lynn & Fakenham Railway in 1882/83.

This is the original M&GN building and running-in board at West Runton, seen in 1990. The buildings have now been replaced.

Beyer-Peacock 4-4-0 No. 23 stands at North Walsham Town station with a freight train.

D16/3 'Super Claud' 4-4-0 No. 62561 arrives at Yarmouth Beach station on 14 July 1951 with a Derby–Lowestoft service. (Ben Brooksbank)

A view looking north at Guestwick on the Norwich City branch in BR days. Points to note are the tablet catching apparatus, the signal box on the platform with a separate cabin for the crossing keeper, and the typical M&GN running-in board with its finials.

Norwich City station was opened by the Lynn & Fakenham Railway in 1882. It was badly bombed in 1942, with the result seen here. Closure to passengers came along with the rest of the system in 1959 but goods traffic continued until 1969.

Sharp Stewart 4-4-0 No. 06 of 1894 waits to depart from Cromer Beach.

The Mundesley branch was opened to freight on 20 August 1898 and to passengers a few days later. The continuation to Cromer was completed in August 1906. There were stations at Paston and Napton, Mundesley, Trimingham, and Overstrand. An initial service of seventeen trains each way was put in place. The Yarmouth–Lowestoft line opened on 13 July 1903. There were stations at Gorleston North, Gorleston-on-Sea, Hopton, Corton, and Lowestoft North. Gorleston Links halt opened in 1914.

In the early 1920s, there were thirteen trains a day between Lowestoft and Yarmouth on the joint line, seven of them provided by the M&GN and six by the GE. Between Peterborough and King's Lynn there were nine services, some running via Spalding. Between Melton and Norwich there were seven trains each way, two of them fast trains Long-distance services consisted of trains or through carriages between King's Cross and King's Lynn, King's Cross and Cromer, and from Birmingham, Manchester, and the Midlands to the coastal resorts and Norwich.

On 17 July 1933, a number of halts were opened on the North Walsham–Yarmouth line. These were at Newtown, Caister Camp, California Cliffs, Scatby, Potter Heigham Bridge, and Sutton Staithe. These halts were generally only open in summer. A Sentinel-Cammell railcar was used for a time to serve them. Sidestrand halt opened on 25 May 1936. From the 1 October 1936 the administration of the M&GN was taken over by the LNE, from which time ex-GE, GC, and GN locomotives started to appear.

Under Nationalisation the M&GN became part of the Eastern Region and its joint existence came to an end. Hellesdon station closed in September 1952 and the Mundesley–Cromer line in April 1953. As a result of its poor condition, the Breydon Viaduct was closed in 1954. Between 1955 and 1957 Diesel Multiple Units took over services on the Mundesley branch, the Melton–Cromer, and the Melton–Norwich lines. Eye Green, Thorney, and Wryde stations closed on 2 December 1957. North Drove closed on 16 September 1958. In that same year the system was considered for closure and, apart from the Mundesley branch, Melton to Sheringham, and the Yarmouth–Lowestoft joint line, this came about on 28 February 1959. In 1960 the Norwich Thorpe to Melton service via North Walsham consisted of ten trains each way daily, taking an hour and a half. On the Mundesley branch there were fourteen trains. These two lines closed in 1964 and the joint line in 1970. A number of sections of line were kept open for freight but all eventually closed, leaving today only the fragment from Newstead Lane Junction–Cromer–Sheringham as part of the national network. There is also the Sheringham–Holt heritage operation.

A busy moment at Bourne in the interwar years. Sharp Stewart Class C 4-4-0 No. 55 waits to depart with a westbound service.

Climbing away from Saxby Junction on the Bourne line is K2/2 2-6-0 No. 61763 with the last Tuesday 'Leicester' on 23 February 1959. (Peter Groom)

A Class 158 DMU passes a derelict Saxby station in 1991. The signal box seen in the background marks the point where the Bourne line branched off.

'Flying Pig' 4MT 2-6-0 No. 43091 is the pilot on a M&GN 'Leicester' near Melton Mowbray troughs in August 1958. (Peter Groom)

A year later in the same location 4F 0-6-0 No. 43937 is in charge of a train heading for M&GN territory. (Peter Groom)

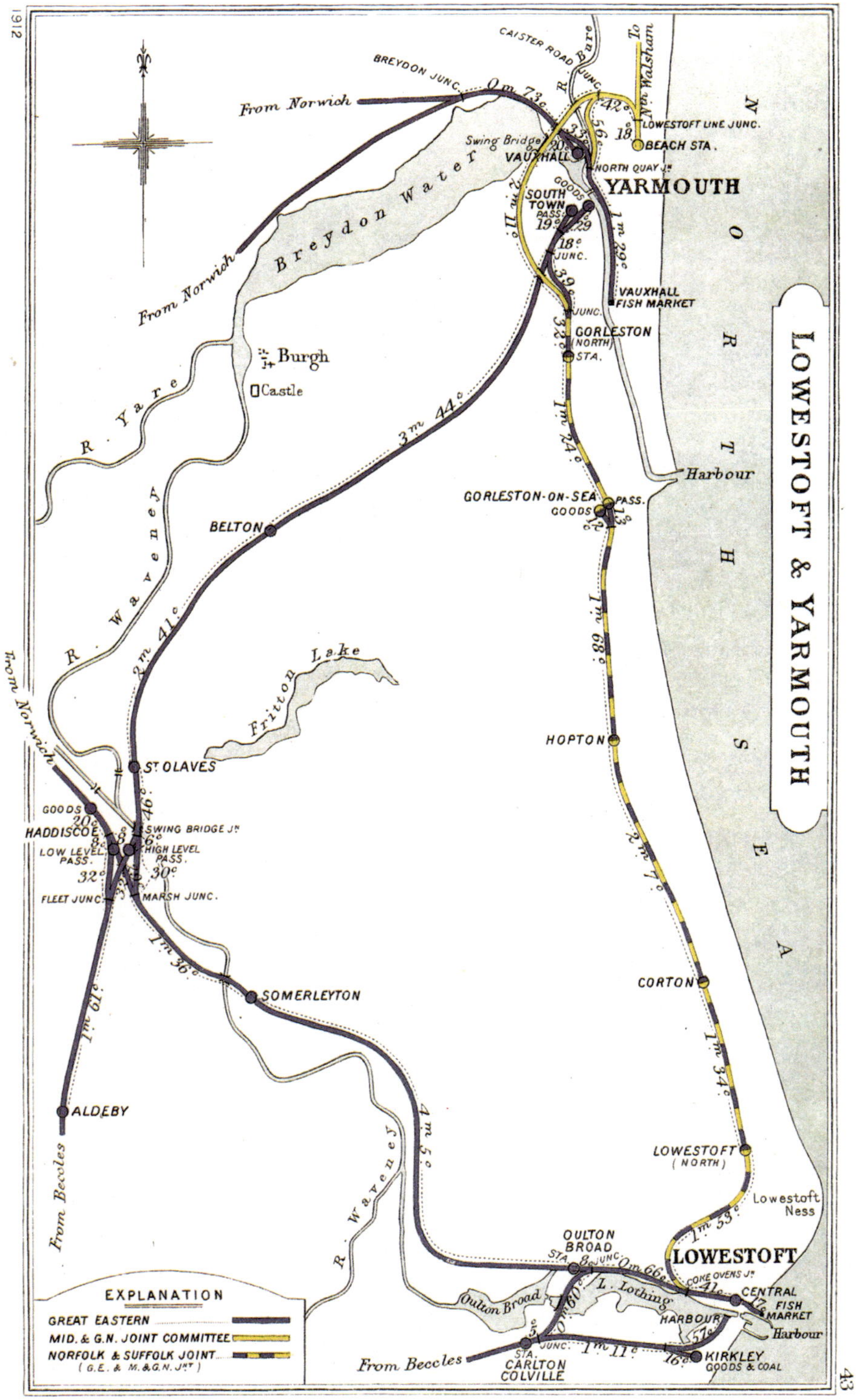


The Norfolk and Suffolk joint line.

Great Eastern F4 2-4-2T No. 186 arrives at Gorleston station shortly after opening.

A view of Corton station taken shortly after opening.

Another Great Eastern train, this time at Mundesley-on-Sea.

Potterheigham Bridge Halt, opened by the joint committee in 1933.

Caister Camp, another halt opened in the same year. The Sentinel steam car will struggle to get all those passengers on board.

## Locomotives and Loco Sheds

On the western lines motive power was provided by the GN and MR. The early railways in the east, the Lynn & Fakenham and the Yarmouth & North Norfolk, had their own engines. Following amalgamation as the Eastern & Midlands Railway the company continued to purchase its own engines. After formation of the M&GN the joint committee bought engines for use on the whole system. These were mainly Midland types. After the takeover by the LNER in 1936, and even more so after Nationalisation, almost any type could be found on the system, though mostly ex-LNER types. In 1950–01 and subsequently the system was allocated a number of Ivatt Class 4 2-6-0s, which then took on much of the work. The main works was at Melton Constable and there were locomotive depots at South Lynn, Norwich, Bourne, Spalding, Yarmouth, and Cromer.

Sharp Stewart 4-4-0 No. 53 of 1894 stands at Norwich City loco depot.

In the late 1930s Class C 4-4-0 No. 55 stands at South Lynn shed.

Johnson 4-4-0 No. 1, built by Sharp Stewart & Co. in 1894 and withdrawn in 1937. It is seen here at Corpusty with a train for Yarmouth.

Nos 41 and 09 4-4-4Ts, built at Melton Works in 1904 and 1909 respectively, seen here receiving attention at the works.

Another Johnson-designed 4-4-0 No. 45 on the turntable at Melton shed. Also present is Kitson 0-6-0 No. 70.

Seen at Melton Constable is ex-Lancaster & Carlisle 2-4-0 No. 43A, built in 1857 and purchased by the Eastern & Midlands Railway in 1883.

# The Great Western & Great Central Joint Line

The GW & GC Joint line started out life as the Wycombe Railway. Authorised by an Act of 1846, its line ran from a junction with the GWR London–Reading main line near the present location of Taplow station. There were stations at Maidenhead Boyne Hill, Furze Platt, Cookham, Bourne End, Wooburn Green, Loudwater, and High Wycombe. Built to the broad gauge, the line was completed by 1854. It was worked from the outset by the GWR. The line at High Wycombe before the new works of the GW & GC line had started. The line was converted to standard gauge in 1870 but the broad-gauge sleepering method was retained.

Frustrated at difficulties encountered sharing the GC & Met Joint line, the GCR came to an agreement with the GWR to build a new joint line. The sections of joint line would be Northolt Junction to Ashendon Junction and Princes Risborough to Aylesbury. The GWR would build its own lines from Northolt Junction to Old Oak Common and from Ashendon Junction to Aynho. The GCR would build a line from Neasden South Junction to Northolt Junction and another from Ashendon Junction to Grendon Underwood Junction, where it would gain access to the previously built London Extension.

In 1897 the GW received authorisation for its new line from Acton to High Wycombe and the following year the GC received its Act for Neasden to Northolt. In 1899 the joint committee was constituted enabling it to absorb the two new lines together with High Wycombe–Princes Risborough. By the same Act the new GC line from Ashendon Junction to Grendon Underwood was authorised. Building work started in 1901 and was completed by 1906, thus giving the GC a better route for its main line to the north. The GW in its turn benefitted from the new arrangements when the Bicester cut-off was completed in 1910, giving it a faster route to Birmingham.

At Neasden South Junction Thomson B1 4-6-0 No. 61369 heads towards London with the 08.30 Manchester London Road to Marylebone on 2 May 1959. In the background on the right is the London Underground depot. The lines to the left are the GW/GC joint lines via Princes Risborough. (Ben Brooksbank)

The same scene thirty years later on 30 May 1989 as a Class 115 DMU, partially repainted in Network SouthEast colours, passes with an Aylesbury–Marylebone service. The signal box is still there and so is the LUL depot, though now obscured by tree growth. A road bridge carrying Great Central Way has been built across the GW/GC lines. The signal box was later removed.

The Great Central used the Metropolitan lines from Quainton Road to Harrow on the Hill, but from the latter location it had its own independent lines into Marylebone. Neasden South is on this section. It was also the junction for the connecting line to the Great Western at Northolt Junction, opened by the GCR in 1906. On 30 May 1989 Brush Type 4, later Class 47, No. 47468 has reversed from the Acton Wells line on to the main line and now sets off to London with its short rake of tanks. Note the rather nice GCR bracket signal.

This is West Ruislip, one of the new stations on the joint line. Like a number of the stations on the new lines, West Ruislip was constructed with two through lines, which it still retained in 1989. One of the through lines was subsequently removed.

Denham Golf Club was opened in 1912 at the request of the local club. On 30 May 1989 a Class 115 unit arrives with an Aylesbury–Marylebone service. Notice the 'Pagoda' cast-iron platform shelters. Once common on the GWR, these are the last surviving pair on the national network. They are listed structures. A number of other stations opened and/or closed over the years.

Loudwater was one of the original Wycombe Railway stations. It closed in 1970. Dorton Halt opened in 1937, Ilmer Halt in 1929, and South Aylesbury Halt in 1933. All closed in 1963.

At Gerrards Cross in 1989 the centre through roads are in the process of being removed. By this time with much-reduced traffic – the loss of through trains to the Midlands and the disappearance of freight – and the need to re-signal, the through lines were felt to be unnecessary. Since that time there has been a resurgence of passenger traffic, with eight trains an hour passing in each direction, as well as freight and special trains.

Seer Green opened as Beaconsfield Golf Links Halt on 1 January 1915. It became Seer Green in 1918, Seer Green and Jordans in 1950, and reverted back to Seer Green in 1974. At Seer Green on 25 March 1950 is the interesting sight of a GC-designed engine running on a GC line that isn't a GC engine at all but rather an ex-GW locomotive! This Robinson-designed 2-8-0 No. 3043 was one of a number built for the Railway Operating Department during the First World War. It was acquired by the GWR in 1925. (Ben Brooksbank)

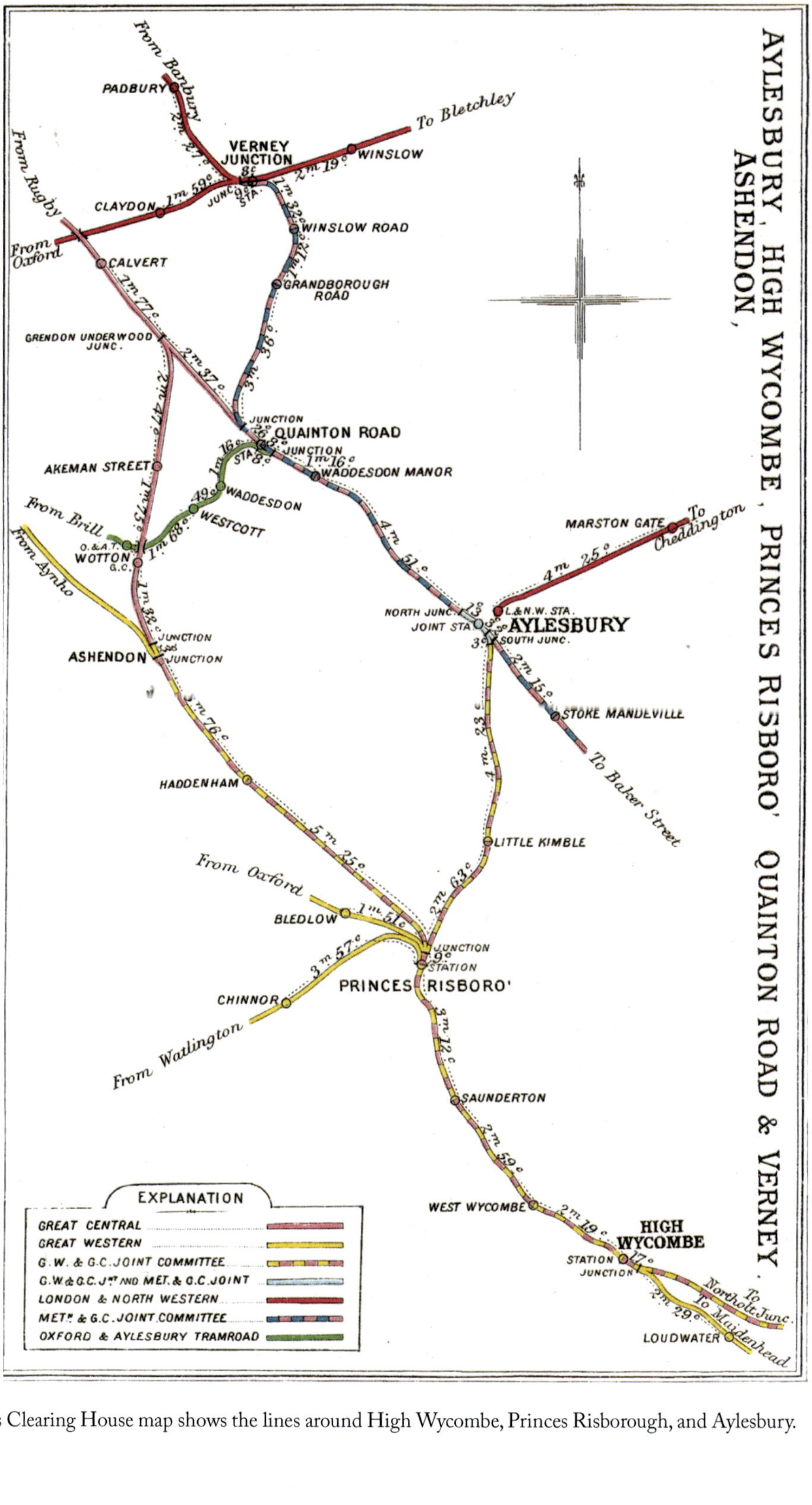


This Clearing House map shows the lines around High Wycombe, Princes Risborough, and Aylesbury.

High Wycombe in 1989. A service for Marylebone stands at the Up platform. On the extreme right is the line for the bay platform and in the foreground the Down platform line. The centre through roads were still extant at this time.

The signals seen in the distance in the previous photograph. On the left is the Up starting signal. The signal for the crossover from Up platform to Up Main has been pulled off for the train which has just departed. On the right is the Inner Home signal.

It is 2015 and the through lines have long gone. At the beginning of that year Chiltern Railways (a subsidiary of DB) surprisingly opted to lease new Class 68s from DRS to replace the Class 67s leased from DB Schenker. Six of the class (Nos 68010–68015) are painted in Chiltern Railways main-line grey livery and equipped to operate with Mk 3 stock and DVTS. On 12 May 2015 Class 68 No. 68015 propels the 15.55 Birmingham Moor Street–Marylebone away from High Wycombe. (Peter Lovell)

Between Saunderton and Princes Risborough is the summit of the GW/GC joint line where the tracks diverge. The southbound line follows a lower profile through a short tunnel and gradients of no more than 1 in 164, while the northbound line descends at 1 in 88 approaching Princes Risborough. On 16 May 2015 preserved Deltic No. D9009 *Alycidon* made a rare appearance with the Belmond British Pullman set on a 07.56 London Victoria–Kidderminster charter to visit the Severn Valley Railway. (Peter Lovell)

After the opening of the new GWR line from Ashendon Junction to Aynho in 1910 Princes Risborough became a busy junction. This new line gave a route between London and Birmingham that was 18½ miles shorter than the old route via Oxford and offered a saving of twenty minutes in journey time. As well as the through route there were branches to Oxford, to Watlington, and to Aylesbury. In this 1989 view looking north, a service is just arriving from Aylesbury. The line to Aylesbury can be seen on the right and the branch to Thame curves round the back of the signal box.

Another photograph taken on the same day shows the single platform in use for both Up and Down trains. On the left is the disused Down platform. The signal box is still active, though reduced to seventy levers.

The same view exactly thirty years later. Much has changed. The Down platform has been brought back into use, connected by a new footbridge. Colour light signalling controlled from Marylebone has replaced the semaphores. The track layout has been much simplified. The signal box has survived and been restored by a group of volunteers. It will eventually control Chinnor & Princes Risborough Railway trains, which currently use the other face of the Down platform. It is also intended that the signal box will act as a museum and be open to visitors.

On 22 September 1956 ex-GW railcar No. W13W stands at the Up platform at Princes Risborough. It is almost certainly engaged on branch-line duty. Between 1934 and 1942 the GWR built thirty-eight of these single railcars, in various configurations. No. W13W dates from 1936. It was powered by a pair of 130-hp AEC engines and could seat seventy. It was withdrawn in 1960.

The same year that No. W13W was withdrawn saw the introduction of its successor, the Class 121 (55000) 'Bubblecar'. These were last used for commercial passenger operations on the national network by Chiltern Railways for the rush-hour services between Princes Risborough and Aylesbury, releasing a Class 165. No. 121034 was owned by the Birmingham Transport Museum and repainted in its original 1960s BR livery. It is seen waiting to depart from Princes Risborough for Aylesbury on the evening of 15 January 2016. Note that the destination blind displays 'Llandudno'! (Peter Lovell)

Fast forward forty years to the introduction of the Class 168/3 units, part of the Class 168 Clubman family. The Class 168/3 units are actually Class 170 units that have been adapted to integrate with the rest of the Chiltern fleet. Each vehicle is powered by a 422-hp MTU diesel engine, giving the unit a top speed of 100 mph. On 30 June 2019 Unit No. 168326 heads a service from Birmingham Moor Street through Princes Risborough.

A view from earlier days as Class 31s Nos 31138 and 31185 head through the station with a Thame to Ripple Lane train of tanks. Note the disused Down platform.

Earlier still, in 1959 ex-GW 0-6-0PT No. 5424 stands at the bay platform having arrived from Aylesbury. (BLS)

# The Metropolitan & Great Central Joint Line

The first railway to open, which was eventually to form part of the Met & GC line, was the Aylesbury & Buckingham, which ran from Aylesbury to Verney Junction, on the Buckinghamshire Railway. It opened in September 1868 and was worked by the GW as an extension of the Wycombe Railway, which had reached Aylesbury in 1863. In 1871 the Duke of Buckingham opened the 6½-mile line to Brill. The Met took over the running of the line in 1899. The Met joined with the St John's Wood Railway to extend the existing railway as far as Harrow, which was reached in 1880. The line was further extended in 1887 by the Harrow & Rickmansworth Railway. Chesham was reached in 1889 and Aylesbury in 1892.

The Manchester, Sheffield & Lincoln Railway (shortly to become the GCR) reached Quainton Road station from the north in 1898. From there it had running powers over the Met as far as Harrow, and from Harrow to Marylebone on its own independent lines. In 1906 the Met lines north of Harrow were leased to a joint committee of the GC and Met for a term of 999 years. This included responsibility for working the Brill Tramway, now known as the Oxford & Aylesbury Tramroad.

Until 1922 the joint line was staffed and maintained for alternating periods of five years by each partner. A branch to Watford was opened in 1925 and this also became part of the joint arrangement. The Brill branch closed in 1935 and the Verney branch lost its passenger service the following year.

Until 1925 the Met & GC line was entirely steam-worked. Locomotive types included Yorkshire Engine Company 'G' Class 0-6-4Ts and 'H' Class 4-4-4Ts. These eight engines were designed by the Metropolitan's Chief Mechanical Engineer Charles Jones and built in 1920/21 by Kerr Stuart and Company. Originally numbered 103 to 110, they were renumbered 6415 to 6422 following the takeover by the LNER of services north of Amersham. They were later moved to other parts of the LNER system before being scrapped in the 1940s. The 'K' Class 2-6-4Ts were introduced in 1925 and spent most of their time on freight work. The Brill branch was worked by a Beyer-Peacock 4-4-0T. The GC local services were handled by 4-4-2Ts. From 1937 the LNER took over responsibility for providing steam haulage for the Met services.

In 1925, electrification was extended to Rickmansworth and Watford, and the former became the changeover point from electric to steam haulage. Electric haulage was by Metropolitan-Vickers 1,200-hp Bo-Bo machines. From 1933 the Met came under the London Passenger Transport Board and part of its New Works Scheme was the electrification to Amersham and Chesham. The Second World War intervened and it was not until 1960 that the electrification was completed. From 1961 the Met trains were in the shape of London Transport 'A' stock units, built by Cravens. These units were in use until 2012 when they were replaced by 'S8' stock, built by Bombardier.

In 1960–61, steam haulage of the GC local services came to an end with the introduction of Class 115 DMUs. These were in turn replaced by Class 165 'Turbo' units in 1990.

Following the extension of electrification to Rickmansworth in 1925, it became the new location for the changeover from electric to steam haulage. Previously this had occurred at Harrow on the Hill. In 1934 Metropolitan H Class 4-4-4T No. 107 stands in the station with a rake of 'Dreadnought' coaching stock.

On 2 September 1961 Metropolitan-Vickers electric locomotive No. 18 *Michael Faraday* heads towards Rickmansworth. It is hauling a rake of 'Dreadnought' carriages. Note the pick-up shoe on the first carriage. This was connected to the locomotive and was fitted to help prevent 'gapping'. The locomotive, one of a class of twenty, was built in 1922/23. These 1,200-hp locomotives had a top speed of 65 mph. All were withdrawn by 1962, after the introduction of 'A' stock multiple units.

Standing at platform 3 at Chalfont and Latimer station in July 1948 is push-pull-fitted Robinson C13 4-4-2T No. 7418 with the Chesham branch service. These Ashbury carriages date from 1898. Between 1906 and 1924 they were converted into Electric Multiple Units. The electrical equipment was later removed when they returned to being hauled vehicles. Two sets of these carriages were used on the Chesham branch. Following electrification of the branch in 1960 one of the sets was sold to the Bluebell Railway where it remains to this day. No. 7418 survived until 1958, completing fifty-five years of service.

Eleven years later the Ashbury coaches are still in use, this time in the charge of Ivatt 2MT 2-6-2T No. 41272, which is propelling the train out of the Chesham branch platform at Chalfont and Latimer. Between 1946 and 1952 130 of this class were built, first by the LMS and then by BR. In 1959 No. 41272 was a 14D Neasden engine. It later went to the Southern Region before ending its days at Skipton, from where it was withdrawn in 1965. (Ben Brooksbank)

Passengers no longer need to change at Chalfont and Latimer as Chesham branch services run direct from either Aldgate or Baker Street. There is a half-hourly service during most of the day. On 4 June 2019 an 'S' stock train sits at the pleasant little station of Chesham. These trains, built by Bombardier, were introduced in 2010. The 3.89-mile Chesham branch opened in 1889. Today the station has just a single platform, but it originally had a bay, which has now been turned into a garden and can be seen on the left.

One year before electrification reached Amersham, on 19 May 1959, Stanier 5MT 4-6-0 No. 45215 stops at the station with the 13.30 stopping service from Marylebone.

A Class 115 DMU forming a Marylebone to Aylesbury service approaches the Metropolitan Railway signal box at Great Missenden. The box was abolished in 1994 and control of the area came under Marylebone IECC. In 2010 the box was moved to the Mid Hants Railway.

Some years earlier, in the 1950s, platform lengthening and other works are being carried out. Note the similarity between the water tower here and the one at Chesham. A steam-hauled freight train waits in the Down loop. The loop no longer exists.

Wendover is deep in the Chiltern Hills and southbound trains have a climb from Aylesbury of nearly 7 miles at up to 1 in 117 before reaching the summit. The line then falls for 4 miles before rising to a second summit at Amersham. At the platform a Class 165/0 unit stands with the 12.57 from Marylebone to Aylesbury Parkway on 3 July 2019.

The GWR opened Aylesbury Town station in 1863. The Aylesbury & Buckingham Railway shared this station from 1868. When the Metropolitan arrived in 1892 it built its own station at Brook Street, but two years later its trains were diverted into Aylesbury Town and Brook Street was closed. The station seen in this photograph dates from 1926, when Aylesbury Town was comprehensively rebuilt.

This photograph of ex-GCR B3 4-6-0 No. 6164 *Earl Beatty* was taken between 1927 and 1939 while No. 6164 and two other members of the class were allocated to Neasden. In 1939 No. 6164 was rebuilt with Caprotti valve gear. This was an attempt to reduce coal consumption in what was one of Robinson's less successful locomotives. No. 6164 is waiting to leave Aylesbury with what was probably an overnight express from Manchester.

At Aylesbury on 22 July 1961 ex-LNER K3 2-6-0 No. 61913 stands with the 16.46 departure to Marylebone. No. 61913 was a 2F Woodford Halse engine at this time and would be withdrawn from that shed just seven months later. The K3s were introduced by Gresley as fast goods engines for the GNR in 1920. They continued to be built by the LNER and altogether a total of 193 were constructed between 1920 and 1937. They had a strangely out-of-proportion appearance due to the 6-foot boilers seeming too large in comparison with the 5-foot 8-inch driving wheels.

A view looking south from Aylesbury station on 30 May 1989 as a Class 115 DMU arrives with a service from Marylebone via Amersham. The line on the right is from Princes Risborough. Work is already under way on resignalling the line, as part of which the tracks here will be remodelled and the signal box abolished.

The long rod attached to the boiler of ex-GC F1 2-4-2T No. 5594 was part of the less than successful mechanical push-pull apparatus fitted in 1922. No. 5594 is seen in LNER days standing at Aylesbury with the motor train for Verney Junction.

Quainton Road station came into being with the opening of the Aylesbury & Buckingham Railway on 23 September 1868, which was worked from the outset by the GWR. In 1891 the A&B was taken over by the Metropolitan Railway, which reached Aylesbury in 1892. Through running between Baker Street and Verney Junction began in 1897. This view looking south dates from the 1930s. Just visible, standing at the Brill platform at the head of a mixed train, is the 4-4-0T Metropolitan A-Class locomotive No. 41 (works No. 865), one of six A-Class engines built by Beyer Peacock in 1869. Note the long line of coal wagons in the background. The grassed enclosure behind the Down platform is a livestock pen.

Quainton Road was closed to passengers on 4 March 1963. Trains on the GCR main line continued to pass through, as here with Stanier 5MT 4-6-0 No. 44920 with the 14.38 Marylebone to Nottingham service on 22 June 1966. Main-line operations ceased later the same year.

Quainton Road station today. In 1962 the London Railway Preservation Society was set up with a base at Quainton Road and later absorbed into the Quainton Railway Society, which now operates the Buckinghamshire Railway Centre. The station has remained largely unchanged since closure and all the buildings including the shelter on the Brill branch platform are listed. Things may change in the future as it is intended that passenger trains will once again run north of Aylesbury as part of the East West Rail Project and a number of changes will have to be made for safety reasons.

Winslow Road was on the A&BR line from Aylesbury to Verney Junction. (The A&BR never did reach Buckingham.) From 1906 services were provided jointly by the GCR and the Met. In 1933 the Met became part of the London Passenger Transport Board, which withdrew passenger services beyond Quainton Road in 1936. The line to Verney Junction closed completely in 1947. On the last day of passenger service ex-GE F7 2-4-2T No. 8307 stands at the station with the autotrain waiting to depart to Verney Junction.

Verney Junction in the 1960s. The lines on the right were previously used by trains coming from the GC/Met joint line from Quainton Road and Aylesbury. That line closed completely in 1947. It turned away from the Oxford–Cambridge line at the far end of the row of carriages. No buildings now remain here, just a pair of overgrown platforms. (Lamberhurst)

A very early photograph of an Aveling and Porter 0-4-0 on the Brill branch hauling an assortment of vehicles, including a four-wheel brake and two cattle wagons. The Wotton Tramway was built to serve the estate of the Duke of Buckingham. The 4-mile-long line to Wotton was in use by 1871, trains originally being horse-drawn. By 1872 the line had been extended a further 2½ miles to Brill and a passenger service started.

Waddesdon station became Waddesdon Road from 1922. At the same time Waddesdon Manor on the Metropolitan/Great Central joint line became Waddesdon. In 1883 the Duke of Buckingham proposed extending the tramway to Oxford and the Act authorising the extension was passed in August that year. The Oxford, Aylesbury & Metropolitan Junction Railway Company was set up, but the investment was not forthcoming. Under the scheme Waddesdon Road station would have disappeared.

In 1894 the tramway was taken over by the Oxford & Aylesbury Tramroad. It was that company which introduced two Manning Wardle K Class 0-6-0 saddle tanks to the line. Seen here at the branch platform at Quainton Road is Brill No. 1 (Manning Wardle No. 1249). At that time the fare from Quainton Road to Brill was sixpence halfpenny and the journey took about forty minutes.

This is Westcott in the 1930s. The train has arrived hauled by one of the Metropolitan Class A tanks. At this time there was a service of four trains on weekdays with an additional service on Saturdays. The journey time was about thirty-two minutes. Trains stopped as required at both Westcott and Wood Siding.

In 1899 the line came under Metropolitan Railway control and in 1903 the Manning Wardle tanks were replaced by two Metropolitan Railway D Class engines. These in turn were replaced by two A Class engines, Nos 23 and 41. These 4-4-0Ts were built by Beyer-Peacock for use on the Metropolitan sub-surface lines. Made redundant by electrification they had their condensing equipment removed and a cab added. No. 41 is seen at Wood Siding. No. 23 survived into preservation and is to be found at the London Transport Museum.

In 1933 the Metropolitan Railway became part of the London Passenger Transport Board and it was decided to terminate all passenger services beyond Aylesbury from 1935. So it was that the Brill branch finally succumbed. The photograph shows the Brill terminus in the last year of service. One of the Class A tanks is at the head of the train.

# The East London Railway

In 1865 the East London Railway was authorised to build a railway from Shoreditch on the GER Liverpool Street line to New Cross (Gate) on the LBSCR main line and to New Cross on the SER line to Hastings, taking over the abandoned Thames Tunnel, built between 1824 and 1843. Wapping to New Cross (Gate) opened on 6 December 1866. There were stations at Rotherhithe and Deptford Road. The ELR had its own station at New Cross adjacent to the LBSCR station. It was the latter company that provided the train service. The initial service was of twenty-three services each way. These trains were worked by two Craven 2-4-0Ts, Nos 51 and 109. Later, Stroudley 0-6-0T 'Terriers' were used.

On 13 March 1871, a 70-chain spur was opened from Dartford Road Junction to Old Kent Road station on the LBSCR South London line. Services ran through to Peckham Rye. By this time there were forty-three trains each way between Wapping and New Cross (Gate). In 1876 spurs to the LBSCR Up line at New Cross (Gate) and to the SER New Cross station were opened. In April of that year the northern part of the line was completed. There were stations at Shadwell, Whitechapel, and Shoreditch. LBSCR trains were able to run into Liverpool Street station and some ran to Croydon.

In 1880, the SER started to run trains between Liverpool Street and Croydon (Addiscombe Road). On 3 March 1884, a spur from the ELR to St Mary's station on the Metropolitan & Metropolitan District Joint line was opened and from 6 October both companies ran through on to the ELR. The Metropolitan trains ran from Hammersmith to New Cross SER, while the Metropolitan District trains ran to New Cross (Gate) LBSCR. In 1882 a joint committee was established to manage the line. The LBSCR, SER, GER, LCDR, Metropolitan District, and Metropolitan were represented. The LBSCR undertook the maintenance of the line. Between 1877 and 1884 there was a service from Liverpool Street to Brighton. In the final two years this consisted of through carriages which were attached at New Cross (Gate). In 1886 the GER took over the running of trains to Liverpool Street station. There were eighteen trains daily between Liverpool Street and Croydon or New Cross, hauled by Worsdell F4 2-4-2Ts.

In 1905, the electrification of the Metropolitan & District Line brought an end to those companies working through onto the ELR. The LBSCR and SER continued to run trains but the latter only at peak times. Services to Peckham Rye ended on 30 June 1911. In 1913 the line was electrified and the Metropolitan provided services to the two New Cross stations. The GER continued to run goods trains. In 1923 the LBSCR station became New

Cross Gate. In 1933 services were taken over by the London Passenger Transport Board. From 1941 services ran from Whitechapel to New Cross and New Cross Gate, extended to Shoreditch in the peaks. In the 1950s there were still steam-hauled freights working through the ELR, mostly in the hands of Holden J67/69 0-6-0Ts. Metropolitan 'F' stock continued to operate the line into the 1960s, being replaced by A60 and A62 stock.

Between 2006 and 2012 the ELR was extended to Highbury and Islington at the northern end, and at the southern end the line from Deptford Road to the former Old Kent Road station was reinstated. The line is now part of the London Overground network and is operated by Class 378 Capitalstar trains. Trains run between Dalston Junction and Clapham Junction or New Cross, and between Highbury and Islington and West Croydon or Crystal Palace.

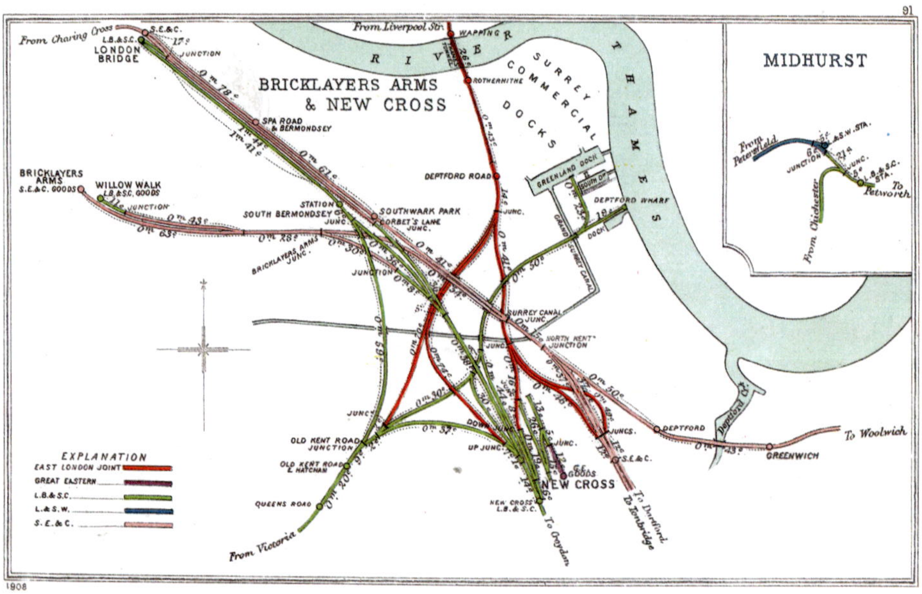


This Clearing House map shows the connections of the ELR at New Cross.

A train consisting of London Underground 'Q' stock arrives at Whitechapel station on 24 July 1970. These vehicles were introduced in 1938 and survived on the ELR until 1971. (Alan Murray-Rust)

Shadwell station, set in a typical East London scene.

Wapping station, dwarfed by dockside warehouses. In this 1930s view the Southern Railway and LNER, successors to the original joint committee members, advertise their services.

Rotherhithe station seen in April 2010. (sunil060902)

A train of 'F' stock at Surrey Canal Junction. In the background is the SECR line from London Bridge.

A train of 'Q' stock at New Cross station in July 1970. (Alan Murray-Rust)

# The Tottenham & Hampstead Junction Railway and the Tottenham & Forest Gate Railway

The Act for the Tottenham & Hampstead Junction Railway was passed on 28 July 1862. Its main purpose was to provide a link between the two systems of the LNWR and GER. The latter agreed to work the line. An Act of 25 July 1864 authorised the MR to build a connection from its London Extension, then under construction, to the T&HJR near Kentish Town. The railway was opened from Gospel Oak to Tottenham North Junction on 21 July 1868. A curve between their Cambridge line and the T&HJR was added by the GER. There were stations at Crouch Hill, Upper Holloway, and Highgate Road. The initial passenger service was between Fenchurch Street station and Highgate Road. There was just one service in each direction daily. The line west of Highgate Road was not used. This passenger service lasted only until January 1870. Earlier that month the MR link between Kentish Town and Highgate Road was opened and the MR and GER agreed to work the line jointly.

The MR trains ran originally from Moorgate Street to Crouch Hill but were extended to South Tottenham when that station opened. The GER trains ran between South Tottenham and St Pancras. In 1876 the connection between the T&HJR and LNWR at Gospel Oak was removed. (During the lifetime of the railway this connection was removed and reinstated no less than three times.) In 1880, the GER built a curve between Seven Sisters and South Tottenham. In 1883 the MR built a new link from Carlton Road Junction to Highgate Road, thereafter enabling trains from the north to proceed directly to the London Docks and other points to the south and east.

Stations were opened at Junction Road and Hornsey Road by 1874, at Harringay Park in 1880, and St Ann's Road in 1883. In 1886 the GER started a passenger service between Highgate Road and Chingford. In 1890, the Tottenham & Forest Gate Railway was authorised. This 6-mile line, jointly promoted by the London Tilbury & Southend and the MR, was opened on 9 July 1894. There were stations at Blackhorse Road, Walthamstow Queen's Road, Leyton, Leytonstone, Wanstead Park, and Woodgrange Park. The MR dealt with ordinary traffic while the LTS ran the trains to Southend, including special boat trains to Tilbury. Before this the GER had run trains to Southend from Gospel Oak via Stratford.

Passenger trains were originally worked by Kirtley 0-4-4WT Nos 690–695 and 780–799. Johnson 0-4-4Ts worked coal trains to South London depots. In 1871 ten Beyer-Peacock 0-6-0Ts, Nos 1610–1619, were built specially for working MR trains through to the London Docks.

In 1895 Upper Holloway enjoyed a service of forty-six Down and fifty-three Up trains on weekdays. The GER ran ten trains a day between Gospel Oak and Chingford. From 1 July 1902 the T&HR became the Tottenham & Hampstead Joint Railway. The MR maintained the railway from Crouch Hill to the west, with the remainder being allocated to the GER. In 1912, following the absorption of the LTS by the MR, the T&FG was no longer a joint line. In 1914 eighty-five passenger trains daily passed along the line, as well as a considerable amount of freight. Highgate Road station closed in 1915. In 1916 the junction at Gospel Oak was reinstated and then removed once more in 1922. By that year the GER were running just three trains daily between Gospel Oak and Tottenham. The MR had a good service between St Pancras and Southend. In March 1940 the junction at Gospel Oak was reinstated once more, the main purpose of which was to provide an alternative route between Feltham and Stratford for freight traffic. A curve between Harringay Park and Harringay Junction was also built at this time. In 1942/43 Junction Road, Hornsey Road, and St Ann's Road stations were closed.

In summer 1953 there was a good service between Kentish Town and Barking. Some services started at St Pancras and eight of these trains ran through to Southend. The 1960 winter timetable shows that the service to Barking was now operated by Class 116 DMUs, with two steam-hauled trains continuing to Southend. In 1962 through trains to Southend ceased with the electrification of the LTS line. In 1981 the Gospel Oak Junction was reinstated once more and the Kentish Town–Barking services now started there. The service was increased from hourly to half-hourly. In 2018 the line was electrified. In 2022 the London Overground service consisted of four trains per hour running between Gospel Oak and Barking, operated by Class 710 EMUs. There was also considerable freight traffic for South Essex destinations.

In the 1980s a Class 101 Metro-Cammell unit arrives at Upper Holloway with a service for Barking. (Martin Addison)

A nineteenth-century view of the exterior of Crouch Hill station.

In the 1950s Harringay Park sees Jinty 0-6-0 No. 47554 pass through with a short freight. The current name for the station is Harringay Green Lanes.

South Tottenham East Junction seen in the 1960s. The lines to the left are the T&FG and those to the right lead to Tottenham South Junction.

The closed Junction Road station is seen in 1951.

Blackhorse Road station is seen in 1961. This station closed in 1981 when a new station was opened to enable interchange with Victoria Line trains.

Class 115 unit L753 arrives at Leytonstone station on 27 June 1992 with the 09.15 Gospel Oak to Barking.

Kirtley 0-4-4WT No. 797, one of the engines used on the T&HJ.

A Johnson '1251' Class 0-4-4T of the type used on the T&HJ. (Ben Brooksbank)

# The West London Railway and the West London Extension Railway

On 21 June 1836, the Birmingham, Bristol & Thames Junction Railway was authorised to build a 3-mile line from the London & Birmingham Railway at West London Junction, near the present site of Willesden Junction station, to the basin of the Kensington Canal near the later Addison Road station. This line crossed the GWR main line on the flat at Wormwood Scrubs. In 1840 the BB&TJR became the West London Railway. The line was initially tried out using the atmospheric system, but this was rapidly abandoned and the conventional line opened on 27 May 1844. It was standard gauge between Willesden and Wormwood Scrubs, then mixed gauge as far as Kensington. There were stations at Great Western Junction and Shepherd's Bush (Uxbridge Road). The initial passenger service consisted of four trains from Kensington to West London Junction and three from Kensington to Great Western Junction. In the other direction there were two from each of West London Junction and Great Western Junction to Kensington. The railway owned just one locomotive and set of carriages. This passenger service lasted only until November of 1844. From 11 March 1845 the line was leased jointly by the GWR and LNWR (successor to the L&B). In 1846 these two obtained powers to double the line and extend it to the Thames. However, nothing happened, nor did it for the next thirteen years.

An Act of 13 August 1859 once again gave the GWR and LNWR powers to double the line and also to bridge over the GWR main line. At the same time, the West London Extension Railway was authorised to build a railway from Kensington to connections with the LSWR and LBSCR at Clapham Junction and to the Victoria & Pimlico Railway at Battersea. The WLER became the joint property of the LNWR, GWR, LBSCR, and LSWR. The section of line from North Pole Junction to Willesden became LNWR property exclusively. The WLER was completed by 1 April 1863. There were stations at West Brompton, Chelsea, and Fulham. A spur from the GWR main line to North Pole Junction enabled the GWR to run trains from Southall to Victoria station. This service continued until 1915. The LNWR started a service from Euston via Addison Road to Crystal Palace. This later became a Willesden–Croydon service.

In 1864, the Hammersmith & City Line made connection with the WLR at Uxbridge Road. In 1869 the LSWR opened the Kensington, Hammersmith & Richmond line, which reached the WLR at Richmond Junction. This line saw no use after 1916 and was lifted. The joint GWR & Central London Railway and Ealing & Shepherd's Bush Railway joined the WLR at Viaduct Junction. This line was only fully completed in 1920.

The WLR was an important freight artery and remains so today. As for passenger services, these were many and various and changed frequently, some only lasting a few years, or even months. Some examples are given below. In 1872 the LNWR started a service from Broad Street to Mansion House via Hampstead, Willesden, Addison Road, and Earls Court. From 1905, following the electrification of the District Line, the trains were hauled by electric locomotives between Earls Court and Mansion House. By March 1911 this service ran only between Willesden and Earls Court. Electrification of the WLR was completed in 1914 and the service was then in the hands of EMUs supplied by Metro-Cammell. In 1922 there were thirty-one trains each way on weekdays. This service was suspended in 1940.

Starting in 1910, the GWR ran a short-lived service between Victoria and Birmingham. In 1912 the LBSCR had a frequent service between Clapham Junction and Addison Road. A train that used the WLR from 1904 until after the Second World War was the Sunny South Special run jointly by the LNWR and LBSCR between Liverpool and the south coast resorts. Today there is a frequent service between Stratford and Clapham Junction and an hourly service between Watford and Clapham Junction. Trains are in the hands of Class 378 EMUs.

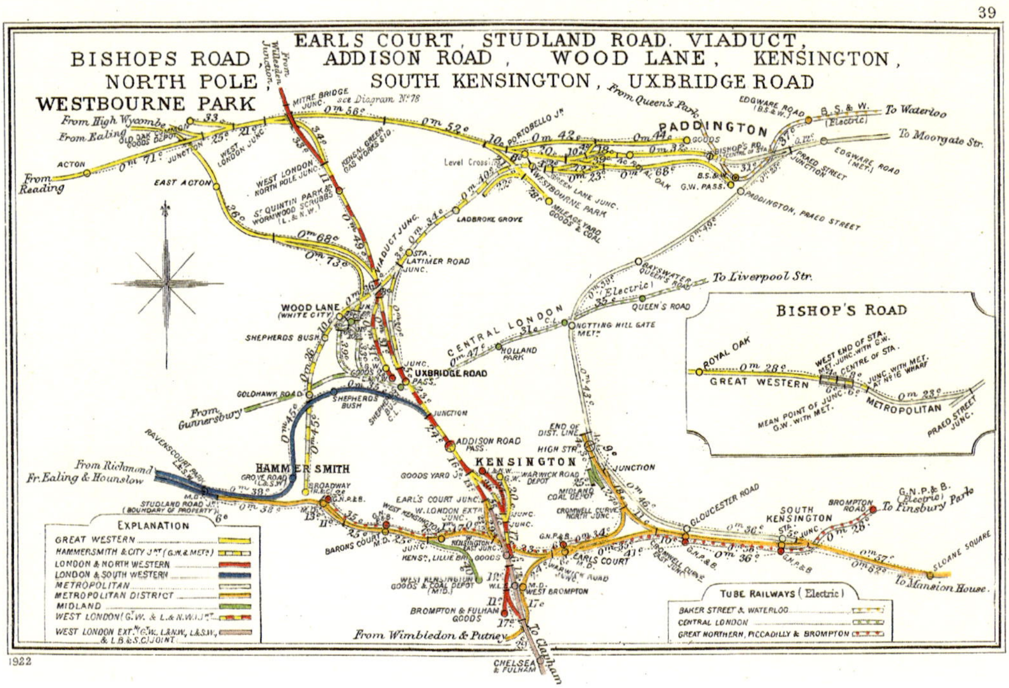


A Clearing House map of the West London and West London Extension Lines.

Addison Road station with the Olympia Exhibition Hall in the background.

An exterior view of Addison Road taken in the 1930s.

LBSC Marsh I1X 4-4-2T No. 12 stands at Addison Road.

Now named Kensington Olympia, on 27 August 2022 the station sees train 6M60 Hanson Aggregates Ardingly to Acton Lane head through hauled by Freightliner Class 66 No. 66556.

On the same day unit No. 378231 stands at the platform with a Stratford to Clapham Junction service.

Uxbridge Road station in the 1930s.

The District Line and WLE stations at West Brompton in 1895.

Chelsea and Fulham station in Southern Railway days with Stroudley D1 0-4-2 No. 338 arriving at the station with a northbound service.

Billinton C2X 0-6-0 No. 32551 comes from the WLE into the Brighton section of Clapham Junction station with a freight train on 2 April 1958. (Ben Brooksbank)

Leaving Clapham junction for Kensington Olympia in 1966 is this unadvertised service which ran a couple of times in the morning and evening peaks. The service ceased in 1968. (Alan Murray-Rust)

# The North & South West Junction Railway

This company was authorised in 1851 to build a double-track line from Willesden to Old Kew Junction on the Hounslow Loop Line. There was a single station at Acton. A passenger service started on 1 August 1853, which from 1858 was provided by the North London Railway. In 1869 the LSWR opened a new line to Richmond and thereafter NSWJ trains ran alternately to Kew Bridge and Richmond. From 1909 the service was provided by the LNWR. The timetable of 1922 shows a regular interval service of four trains an hour from Broad Street, with extra trains in the peak. Today there is a service of four trains per hour running between Richmond and Stratford. The line remains an important freight artery.

On 1 May 1857, a branch to Hammersmith and Chelsea station was opened. This line left the NSWJ at the north-facing Acton Gate House Junction. For many years the branch

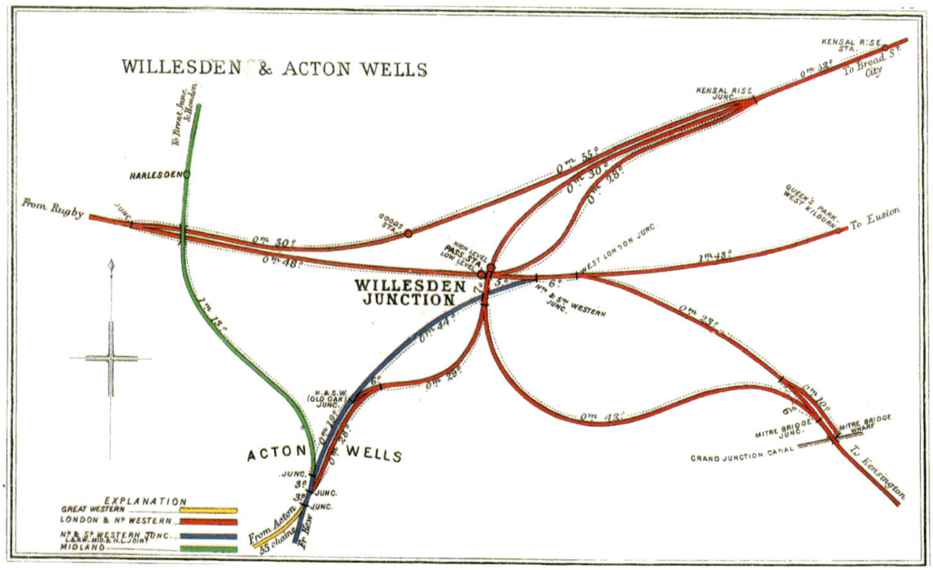


The northern section of the NSWJ.

was worked by NLR 4-4-0T Nos 107 and 108, but from 1909 LNW steam railmotors were used. In the face of tram competition, halts were opened at Rugby Road, Woodstock Road, and Bath Road but to no avail and the passenger service ended on 1 January 1917. On 2 January 1860, the NSWJ was joined at Old Oak Junction by the Hampstead Junction Railway. The Midland & South Western Junction Railway provided the link between the NSWJ at Acton Wells Junction and the MR main line near Cricklewood. This line opened on 1 October 1868 and became part of the MR in 1874. Also joining at Acton Wells junction was a spur from the GWR main line. From 1871 the NSWJ was leased jointly to the LNWR, MR, and NLR. South Acton station opened on 1 January 1880. Acton became Acton Central on 1 November 1925.

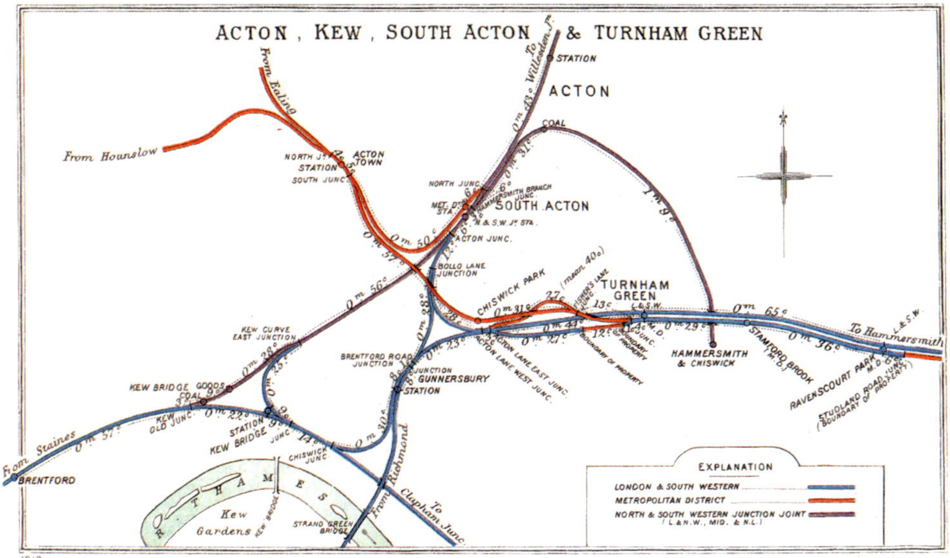


The southern section of the NSWJ.

Heading South near Acton Wells Junction on 23 April 1955 is Q1 No. 33018 with a mixed freight. (Ben Brooksbank)

Park 4-4-0T No. 14 with a NLR service for Richmond.

One of the LNW steam railmotors at Woodstock Road. These machines had been introduced in 1905. They were powered by a two-cylinder engine driving the leading bogie. The engine and bogie could be removed as one unit when maintenance was needed. They had a seating capacity of forty-eight.

North London Railway Adams 4-4-0T No. 107, which was built in 1865 and rebuilt in 1904. It worked for many years on the Hammersmith branch.

A single 1923 'G' stock unit stands at Acton South station with the shuttle from Acton Town. This service was withdrawn in 1959.

A modern view of Acton South station. The District Line platform was alongside to the left, where there are now blocks of flats. (Dr Neil Clifton)

# The Woodside & South Croydon Railway

This railway, which ran from a junction with the Croydon (Addiscombe Road) branch to Selsdon on the Oxted line, was authorised on 6 August 1860 and subsequently acquired jointly by the LBSCR and the SER. It opened on 10 August 1885 and was worked for alternate twelve-month periods by the two owning companies. There was just one intermediate station, at Coombe Lane. In 1895 there was a service of ten trains daily in each direction. In 1905, a single-class railmotor service was introduced and halts opened at Bingham Road and Spencer Road. In 1912 there was a service of eighteen or nineteen trains on weekdays only. This service was suspended on 1 January 1917.

The line was electrified and a half-hourly passenger service reinstated from 30 September 1935. Spencer Road halt was demolished and Bingham Road upgraded to a station. Coombe Lane was renamed Coombe Road. By 1950 there were through trains to London only in the peaks, and in 1976 through trains were withdrawn altogether. The line closed completely on 13 August 1983.

In 1983, shortly before closure, unit No. 4165740 is seen at Coombe Road station. (Lamberhurst)

Bingham Road station is seen in 1963 with EPB unit No. 5747 at the platform. (Lamberhurst)

The view north at Selsdon Road station in May 1983. The line on the right leads to the goods yard. (Lamberhurst)

# The Croydon & Oxted Railway

The Croydon & Oxted Railway was a joint enterprise of the LBSCR and SER. It ran from South Croydon Junction to Crowhurst South Junction, where it made connection with the SER Redhill–Tonbridge line. The line from Crowhurst North to East Grinstead was entirely LBSCR property. Both lines opened on 10 March 1884. There were stations at Sanderstead, Upper Warlingham, and Oxted. Woldingham opened in 1885, Hurst Green halt in 1907, and Riddlesdown in 1927. There were considerable engineering works and steep gradients on the line as it cut through the chalk of the North Downs. These works included Riddlesdown Viaduct and the 1-mile 50-chains Oxted Tunnel.

Up until 1914 the line was busy, with forty-nine Down and forty-three Up trains at Oxted, the majority LBSCR. This number was reduced during the First World War by withdrawal of the SECR services. In 1922 twenty-nine Down and twenty-eight Up LBSCR trains called at Oxted. The SECR had just two Up services between London Bridge and Tonbridge using the line and one Down. In 1962 Diesel Electric Units were introduced to the line and in 1987 it was electrified through to East Grinstead. Today there is a basic half-hourly service between Victoria and East Grinstead with a few services running via London Bridge to the Midland main line. The Uckfield trains also use this route but do not stop at intermediate stations on the C&O.

At Sanderstead on 23 May 1973 4EPB No. 5259 stands with a southbound service. (Lamberhurst)

An early view of Woldingham station.

Hurst Green Halt seen probably shortly after opening. The halt was served only by railmotors, as seen in the photograph. In 1961 the halt closed and a new Hurst Green station was opened further north.

In June 1977 'Thumper' DEMU No. 1304 passes a Class 33 as it enters Oxted station. (Lamberhurst)

A scene from 1985 as Riddlesdown Viaduct is crossed by a train consisting of three 'Thumper' DEMUs. (Lamberhurst)

# The Tooting, Merton & Wimbledon Railway

The TM&W was authorised on 29 July 1864 to build a line from the LSWR at Wimbledon to the LBSCR at Streatham via Haydons Road and Tooting, and a second line from Wimbledon to Tooting via Merton Park and Merton Abbey. The West Croydon to Wimbledon line had previously opened in 1855. The joint committee took over the section of this line between Merton Park and Wimbledon. The TM&W was vested jointly in the LBSCR and LSWR on 5 July 1865 and opened on 1 October 1868. LBSCR had services on both lines, while the LSWR restricted itself to the Haydons Road branch. All services were withdrawn on 1 January 1917 as a wartime economy measure. Services were restored on 27 August 1923 and the Haydons Road line was electrified on 3 March 1929. On the same day passenger services between Tooting and Wimbledon via Merton Abbey were withdrawn. This line remained open for goods traffic until 1975.

This is the first Tooting Junction station, superseded by a second station opened in 1894. After this date the building became the station master's house.

A pair of 4SUB units stand at Merton Park station. Merton Park was originally named Lower Merton.

In Southern Railway days an M7 0-4-4T stands with its train at Merton Abbey.

# The Epsom & Leatherhead Railway

The Epsom & Leatherhead Railway was built by an independent company but from 1863 was vested jointly in the LBSCR and LSWR. At Epsom each had its own station. The LBSCR was to the east of that of the LSWR and to reach Leatherhead passed through the centre two roads of the LSWR station. Initially, the station at Leatherhead was shared but when the Brighton Company extended its line to Dorking in 1867 it made a deviation and built its own station. In 1925 the line was electrified. In 1927 the LSWR station at Leatherhead was closed and all trains used the former LBSCR station. In 1929 the former LSWR station at Epsom was rebuilt as a four-platform station and the LBSCR station of Epsom Town was closed. There is an intermediate station at Ashtead.

The LSWR Epsom station with a train arriving from the Wimbledon direction. The LBSCR lines curve away to the right.

In 1911 Billinton B2X 4-4-0 No. 314 stands with its train at Ashstead station.

The LSWR station at Leatherhead. The first LBSCR station was to the north. The second station was built on the branch to Dorking.